WALKS FOR ALL AGES
DEVON

WALKS FOR ALL AGES

DEVON

RACHAEL ROWE

BRADWELL
BOOKS

Published by Bradwell Books
9 Orgreave Close Sheffield S13 9NP
Email: books@bradwellbooks.co.uk

1st Edition

ISBN: 9781909914919

Print: Gomer Press, Llandysul, Ceredigion SA44 4JL

Design by: Andrew Caffrey

Typesetting by: Mark Titterton

Photograph Credits: © Rachael Rowe, iStock and creative commons

Maps: Contain Ordnance Survey data
© Crown copyright and database right 2014

Ordnance Survey licence number 100039353

The information in this book has been produced in good faith and is intended as a general guide. Bradwell Books and its authors have made all reasonable efforts to ensure that the details are correct at the time of publication. Bradwell Books and the author cannot accept any responsibility for any changes that have taken place subsequent to the book being published. It is the responsibility of individuals undertaking any of the walks listed in this publication to exercise due care and consideration for the health and wellbeing of each other in the party. Particular care should be taken if you are inexperienced. The walks in this book are not especially strenuous but individuals taking part should ensure they are fit and able to complete the walk before setting off.

CONTENTS

Walk 1	Appledore	4 miles	p.10
Walk 2	Beer	3 miles	p.14
Walk 3	Bigbury-on-Sea	3 miles	p.20
Walk 4	Bishop's Tawton	3 miles	p.24
Walk 5	Chudleigh	4 miles	p.28
Walk 6	Colyton	3½ miles	p.32
Walk 7	Dartington	4 miles	p.36
Walk 8	Dittisham	3 miles	p.40
Walk 9	Great Torrington	4 miles	p.44
Walk 10	Hartland	5 miles	p.50
Walk 11	Hembury Woods	2 miles	p.54
Walk 12	Lee	2 miles	p.58
Walk 13	Otterton	3 miles	p.62
Walk 14	Plymouth	2 miles	p.66
Walk 15	Salcombe	4 miles	p.72
Walk 16	Start Point	2 miles	p.76
Walk 17	Tiverton	3 miles	p.80
Walk 18	Uffculme	2 miles	p.84
Walk 19	Westward Ho!	4 miles	p.88
Walk 20	Whimple	4 miles	p.92

INTRODUCTION

Ancient green lanes, mystical moorland trails and dramatic clifftop paths draw walkers to Devon each year, captivated by the beauty of the county. This is diverse walking country where sea spray and rich farmland combine to form some of the finest trails in England. Devon is home to the Tarka Trail and the South West Coast Footpath but has many smaller walks packed with history, views, and culture.

Devon is inspirational to writers. In Dittisham and Bigbury-on-Sea Agatha Christie created crime scenes and compelling characters. The rushing waters of the Torridge formed the setting for Henry Williamson's *Tarka the Otter*. When Victorian readers absorbed the descriptions of the North Devon coast an entire resort sprang up at Westward Ho! to accommodate visitors inspired by Charles Kingsley. Devon's rich nautical heritage is renowned. In Plymouth there are walks past pubs frequented by press gangs and connections to famous ships. There are shipwrecks too and walks along coastal paths once dominated by wreckers. It is all too easy to wander a path at Hartland or Lee Bay and imagine what it must have been like as a smuggler sneaking furtively up these trails with kegs of brandy 200 years ago.

Waking in Devon is one of the finest ways of getting to know the county, from exploring a small village like Whimple to wandering through ancient woodland. The Devon countryside has much to offer walkers and is renowned for its deceptive hills that are steeper than they look. But there's a reward at the end of a Devonian walk that goes beyond a tempting tearoom or a dip in the sea. It is the feeling of getting under the skin of a place by wandering the trails and spending time observing nature, seeing local traditions, and learning about the history as they combine to create a captivating walk.

APPLEDORE

WALK HEADS OUT THROUGH THE OLD SHIPBUILDING AREAS OF APPLEDORE AND ALONG THE RIVER TORRIDGE BEFORE HEADING BACK ALONG THE ESTUARY VIA NORTHAM BURROWS COUNTRY PARK AND THE LIFEBOAT STATION TO THE VILLAGE.

Appledore is located where the Rivers Taw and Torridge meet and has a long shipbuilding tradition with some of the heritage dating back to medieval times. During the reign of Elizabeth I both Appledore and neighbouring Bideford were two of the largest tobacco importers. Many of the houses in the village date back to Tudor times. The shipping industry was at its height in the nineteenth century with the foundation of the Appledore Yard in 1855. Richmond Dry Dock was built in 1856 by William Yeo. Many renowned ships were built here with work continuing until the 1960s. Today there is one shipbuilder left and a museum in the village tells the history of seafaring in Appledore. In Charles Kingsley's novel **Westward Ho!**, Appledore is described as a 'little white fishing village'. A walk around its historic streets with pastel-coloured houses reveals quaint galleries, narrow alleyways leading to courtyards, and Appledore Quay which remains at the heart of the community.

THE BASICS

Distance: 4 miles / 6.4km

Gradient: Mainly level with some uphill parts

Severity: Easy

Approx. time to walk: 3 hours

Stiles: Four

OS Maps: OS Explorer 139 (Bideford, Ilfracombe & Barnstaple)

Path description: Road, footpath and coastal path. Tide times should be checked before walking this route as it is best completed at low tide

Start point: Car park off Churchfield Road (GR SS 465307)

Parking: Off Churchfield Road (EX39 1RL). Parts of this car park can flood at very high tides. Be aware of tide times and watch out for warning signs. Remember to allow for the time you will be away walking

Dog Friendly: Keep dogs on leads on the road

Public toilets: Car park off Churchfield Road

Nearest food: Several places to eat in Appledore including the Coffee CabinHockings Ice cream is made locally and is only available in North Devon

1. Walk out of the Churchfields Car Park and along Appledore Quay. There are lovely views across the water here. Continue past the row of shops and cafés to the Richmond Dock. This was a historic dry dock where many ships were built until the shipbuilding yard relocated to Torridge. On the wall is a list of all the ships constructed here from trawlers to ice breakers. There is also a brief history of the dry dock itself.

2. At the road junction take the road around to the left. Continue up the hill until there is a footpath sign on the left.

3. Take this path, which leads downhill, and then around to the left before progressing ahead with views of the village. This path emerges onto a lane. Ahead is a footpath between a wall. Go along this path, which leads towards the water and is partially on a boardwalk.

4. Walk along the path to the right and along the estuary edge. At high tide this may not be passable. Tide times must be consulted before walking this route.

5. Just before reaching a small beach there is a path leading uphill on the right. Go up this lane and follow the track uphill and around to the left, and onwards to the road.

6. At the road junction on the left there is a memorial to Bloody Corner. This marks the spot where Viking King

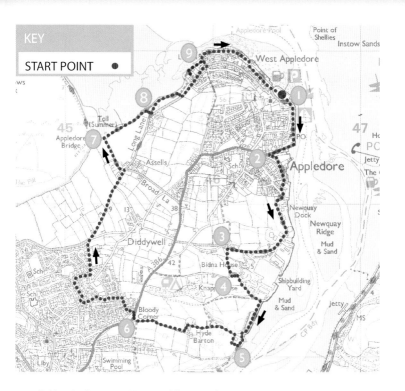

Hubba the Dane was killed by Alfred the Great in AD 892. Walk across the road to the housing estate named J.H. Taylor Drive. Walk through this estate and at the junction with Diddywell Road turn right. Walk through the second group of houses named Lily Close. At the Highbury Hill junction turn left. Walk up this road and at the junction turn right into Long Lane. When you reach a distinctive corner house with curved walls turn left along Burrows Lane, which leads to Northam Burrows Country Park.

7. At the cattle grid turn right and continue along the footpath which runs along the shore. Walk along the path to some steps on the right leading to the South West Coastal Footpath.

8. Take this path to the left. It curves to the right and then meets up with the road. Turn left and walk down this road towards Appledore. At the sign marked lifeboat station turn left. Walk down this road where you can spend time at the RNLI station to see the lifeboat, learn about its history and see how the volunteer crew save lives.

9. Go back along the coast path to the right and follow the streets past the coloured cottages to the car park and the end of the walk.

BEER

This walk leads through the picturesque village of Beer and uphill to the Pecorama Gardens before heading through the surrounding countryside to Beer Caves and then returning to the beach.

Beer lies on the East Devon part of the Jurassic Coast in Lyme Bay and is renowned for its pebble beach dotted with fishing boats. The village is full of beautiful cottages, souvenir shops and cafés, and is popular with holidaymakers. Beer Village is also known for lace

making and lots of examples of this traditional craft can be seen in the shops. Just above the village are the Pecorama Gardens, home to a number of quaint model railways which are a fun diversion on the walk.

Beer Caves is a major attraction in this area. Visiting them is like stepping back in time over thousands of years. Valued by stonemasons, Beer stone is prized for its quality. It is soft to carve when first quarried and hardens on exposure to air. Quarrymen have worked here since Roman times and Beer stone features in many monuments including Winchester Cathedral, Colyton Church and Exeter Cathedral. One of the centrepieces in the caves is a medieval stone carving for a church. The caves are full of history, including secret chapels

for Catholic worship during the Reformation, tales of illicit smuggling hideouts, and 17th-century carvings in the walls. During World War II the caves served as a munitions store. Generations of Beer people are connected with the caves and they were once a major employer in the area. Quarrying stopped here in 1920 with the opening of another quarry. Today the caves are open for guided tours and make an interesting detour on this walk.

THE BASICS

Distance: 3 miles / 4.8km

Gradient: One steep uphill walk out of the village. Otherwise the walk is fairly level

Severity: Easy

Approx. time to walk: 2–3 hours depending on how long visitors spend at the attractions en route

Stiles: none

OS **Maps:** OS Explorer 116 (Lyme Regis & Bridport)

Path description: About 75 per cent on roads and tracks, the remainder field walking

Start point: Central Long Stay Car Park, Clapps Lane (GR SY 229892)

Parking: Central Long Stay Car Park, Clapps Lane (EX12 3EL)

Dog Friendly: Not allowed in the caves. Otherwise they should be kept on leads near roads. Locals have left signs up near woodland at point 5 warning of adders and advising dog owners to keep dogs on leads

Public toilets: South end of Fore Street

Nearest food: Lots of choice around the town

BEER WALK

1. Walk from the car park in Beer, downhill towards the village. Turn right and head into the main street. Follow the road to the right and through the village towards the beach. At the Anchor Hotel turn right and walk up Common Lane. This road weaves up the hill and is steep but there are lots of strategically placed seats along the way. At the top is a car park.

2. Turn right onto Southdown Road. At its junction with Clapps Lane turn left. Almost immediately there will be a footpath with a central handrail leading uphill to Barline, then on to Underleys. At Underleys, turn right and walk downhill to its junction with Mare Lane.

3. Follow Mare Lane as far as Pecorama Gardens. This is an optional stop on the walk. To the left of the car park is a marked public footpath. Follow this path on the left. Eventually this emerges at a farm track. Walk along this track and turn right at a junction in the path.

4. Continue walking on the farm track to a footpath sign on the right. The marker for this sign is almost opposite a footpath gate entrance on the left. Take the path on the right, which leads across a field through a kissing gate to a wooded area.

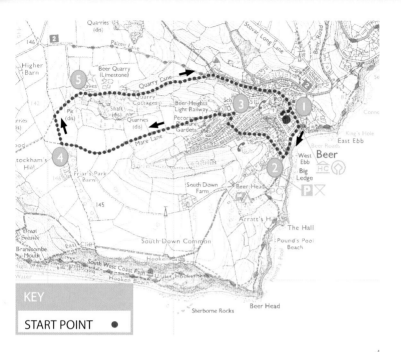

KEY

START POINT ●

Local residents have left signs warning of adders in the area. Dogs should be kept on a lead, and walkers should stay on the path. Follow the path through the woods which leads to Beer Caves. There is an option to stop here and take a guided tour. The tours run daily at specified times which are displayed on the website (www. beerquarrycaves.co.uk) and also at the entrance. There is also a small café here during opening times.

5. Take the path out of Beer Caves car park and turn right. This road leads back to Beer past picturesque cottages. In the village there are options to visit one of the cafés, spend time at the museum, or buy freshly caught fish from the local fishermen on the beach.

Appledore

Beer

Bigbury

BIGBURY-ON-SEA

This walk starts at the beach in Bigbury-on-Sea and goes uphill across fields and through a golf course with views across the River Avon. The walk returns to Bigbury-on-Sea via a nature reserve and the beach. It can easily be combined with a side trip to Burgh Island.

Bigbury-on-Sea has a popular sandy beach, attracting visitors for its rock pools, swimming, surfing and other water sports. Its most famous landmark is Burgh Island with its iconic art deco hotel. At high water Burgh Island is surrounded by sea and accessible only by sea tractor. During low tide a sandy causeway appears. Visitors can walk to the island from the beach at low water but need to keep an eye on the incoming tide.

Stephen McKay

Burgh Island was once known as La Burgh and had a huer's hut used to alert villagers to pilchard shoals. The Pilchard Inn dates from the 14th century and was used by monks and fishermen as well as being a smugglers' bolthole. It is also reputed to be haunted. During the 1920s Burgh Island was bought by Archibald Nettlefold, who built the hotel and used it as a guest house for celebrities and friends. Burgh Island was visited by Edward VIII and Mrs Simpson, Noel Coward and Agatha Christie. Two of Agatha Christie's books, **And Then There Were None** and **Evil Under the Sun**, were inspired by or written on Burgh Island. During the 1990s the Burgh Island Hotel was restored to its original art deco splendour by Tony Porter and is now a luxury hotel.

The South West Coast Footpath also runs through Bigbury-on-Sea.

THE BASICS

Distance: 3 miles / 4.8km

Gradient: One steep ascent and descent

Severity: A pleasant walk with steep parts

Approx. time to walk: 2 hours

Stiles: Four

Maps: OS Explorer OL20 (South Devon)

Path description: Footpaths, road, beach

Start point: Marine Drive Car park (GR SX 651443)

Parking: Marine Drive, Bigbury-on-Sea, TQ7 4AS. In summer there is an economy car park on the walking route opposite Mount Folly Farm. The postcode for that is TQ7 4AR

Dog Friendly: Must be kept on a lead on the road and golf course

Public toilets: Next to The Venus Café (on the Bigbury-On-Sea car park)

Nearest food: Venus Café, The Pilchard Inn, Bay Café. Another possibility is to take a trip to Burgh Island

BIGBURY-ON-SEA WALK

1. Begin the walk from the car park and walk uphill to the footpath marked Chiselborough. Follow this path around to the left and then uphill past some houses.

2. At the end of this road cross over a stile. A footpath leads uphill through a field. The path leads through a permissive route and has beautiful views of Bigbury-on-Sea and Burgh Island.

3. Continue walking uphill past evidence of disused World War II gun emplacements and some old stone walls. In World War II the area was heavily defended as there was concern the Germans would use Burgh Island as a beachhead to invade the mainland. The path leads to a second field through a gate and towards a stile to a lane.

4. Turn left and follow the lane to the road, which curves round to the right. Walk down this road, which has lovely views of the countryside to the left.

5. At the golf course turn right and continue along the footpath. This goes through the golf course itself and walkers must keep to the marked trail which leads downhill. Keep a look out for golfers teeing off. There are beautiful views of the Avon ahead and to the left. Follow this trail as it curves round to the left of the golf course and continues downhill.

6. Take the footpath to the left through a field towards some trees. Just before the trees turn right and follow the path downhill. This is very steep and care should be taken when walking. Go through two stiles.

7. At the bottom of the slope turn right and walk along the path through Cockleridge Ham. In summer there is a small ferry that runs from here to Bantham. Watch out for large rabbit holes underfoot and along the path. Follow this path to the right and then uphill to the left.

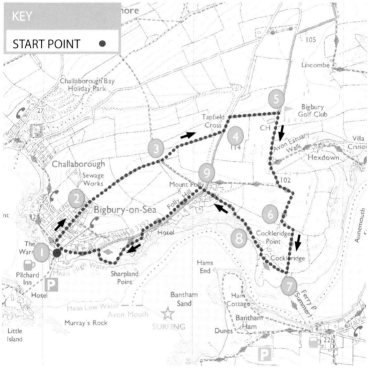

8. The path runs close to the cliff edge and is a steep climb uphill. At the top there is a beautiful view point across the bay and the estuary. There is also a thoughtfully placed seat to enjoy those sea views.

9. Walk ahead past Mount Folly Farm and cross the road to the footpath. This footpath leads downhill towards the beach through a field which doubles as an economy car park in summer. Depending on the tide take either the road or the beach to the right returning to the car park where the walk commenced.

BISHOP'S TAWTON

This walk begins in Bishop's Tawton and heads out up Codden Hill to a panoramic viewpoint. It returns steeply to Bishop's Tawton with views of the famous whaleback hills that are iconic in this part of Devon.

Bishop's Tawton lies in the valley of the River Taw surrounded by farmland and is just a few miles from Barnstaple. The area around Codden Hill is famed for the whaleback hill formations which can be seen as far as Swimbridge. These distinctive shapes in the landscape occurred as a consequence of tectonic plates colliding around 300 million years ago. Codden Hill is the most dramatic of the whaleback hills in this area and has magnificent views from the beacon. These stretch as far as Hartland, Bodmin Moor, Dartmoor and Exmoor on a clear day. The monument on the beacon was established by the late Jeremy Thorpe, the North Devon MP, in memory of his wife who died in 1970. Today it is a beautiful spot for a picnic, flying a kite or simply enjoying a magnificent Devon view. The toposcope at the monument lists 18 viewpoints to see. The permissive routes around Codden Hill are a designated Natural England Conservation Walk.

Bishop's Tawton has a collection of interesting buildings, many dating back to medieval times. It is one of the earliest residences of the Bishop of Exeter, who was based here until Tudor times, hence its name. Bishop's Tawton was home to the suffragette Clara Codd, who was born in the village in 1877. There are two pubs which date from the 17th century and the village has Victorian almshouses as well as a number of pretty cottages.

THE BASICS

Distance: 3 miles / 4.8km

Gradient: Steep ascents and descents

Severity: This is a fairly easy walk but has steep ascents and descents

Approx. time to walk: 2 hours

Stiles: None

Maps: OS Explorer 139 (Bideford, Ilfracombe & Barnstaple)

Path description: Road, woodland track, path

Start point: Chichester Arms, Village Street (GR SS 567300)

Dog Friendly: Near the Chichester Arms (EX32 0DQ)

Parking: Keep on a lead near livestock and on the road

Public toilets: None

Nearest food: Chichester Arms, The Three Pigeons

1. Start at the Chichester Arms and walk up Village Street with the pub on your right. Turn right by the Chichester Arms, passing a tree and a bench, towards Codden. Walk up the hill to Sentry Lane.

2. Continue following this lane past houses and with views of the farmland on the left. The road curves round to the right. At the corner where it curves again is a lane leading uphill. Take this lane. Walk along this footpath, which goes slightly uphill and curves around a wooded area.

Continue walking along the path. In the distance ahead is the distinctive white building of Tawstock Court, built by Sir Bourchier Wrey in 1787. This became Tawstock School from the 1940s but all but the nursery school closed in 2011.

3. Look for a sharp uphill track on your left. Go up this footpath which leads steeply uphill through deciduous trees. Continue along the path where there are views of the quarry on the left and the other whaleback-shaped hills. This path continues to a stone path leading steeply uphill. Take this trail to the top. Turn to the right and continue upwards towards a bench which makes a welcome break and affords superb views. Keep walking as there are more panoramic scenes to come.

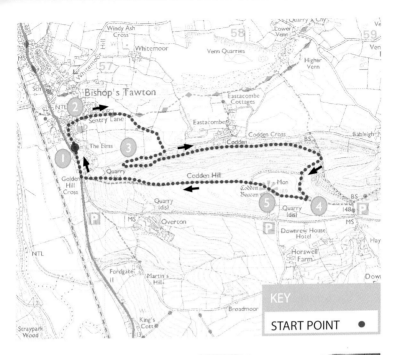

KEY

START POINT ●

4. Walk onwards and to the right, taking the footpath towards the beacon. The views here are worth the climb and on a clear day stretch for miles out to sea and across moorland. There is also a Bronze Age bow barrow just below the monument with a ditch.

5. After admiring the views walk past the monument to a gate. Go through the gate to a footpath and continue walking downhill with some beautiful views to the side and ahead. This path descends very steeply for the final part of the route and care needs

to be taken when walking on this trail. At the bottom of the hill walk through the kissing gate to the road. Turn right and walk up to Village Street. This takes you back into Bishop's Tawton where the walk began.

CHUDLEIGH

This walk starts in the small market town of Chudleigh and heads out along lanes past part of an Iron Age settlement. The walk returns to the town via Chudleigh Rocks; a unique attraction with caves and gardens.

Chudleigh might be a small town in mid Devon but it has over a thousand years of history. It has Saxon origins and following the Norman Conquest the town grew in importance. During the 14th century Chudleigh was granted a charter fair. Chudleigh grew up around the wool trade and was a prosperous place but in 1807 a fire destroyed two-thirds of the town. Today there are many walks within a few miles of Chudleigh and it is ideal for outdoor activities.

Chudleigh Rocks was a quirky Victorian attraction and was formed from a huge outcrop of Devon limestone. Visitors came to climb to the summit of the rock and admire the magnificent view across the Teign Valley. The more adventurous visitors would explore the caves armed with a pin, which was to be placed in a stalagmite formation, called the 'Pope's Head', as a means of warding off mischief by the pixies who were reputed to live there. A quarry was established near Chudleigh in 1080 to provide stone for a Bishop's Palace. Today just a few old walls remain with most having been dismantled over the

years. In 1845 Rock House was built and the gardens and rock gardens followed. Today visitors can explore the rock formations, visit the caves and wander around the gardens. There are luscious palm trees in the remains of the Bishop's Palace, which is now named 'Little Africa', and a number of winding paths lead to caves, grottoes and beautiful viewpoints.

THE BASICS

Distance: 4 miles / 4.6km

Gradient: Undulating

Severity: Easy

Approx. time to walk: 2 hours with additional time needed to visit Chudleigh Rocks. There is a small admission charge to Chudleigh Rocks and opening times can be checked via the website (www.therockgardens.co.uk)

Stiles: None

Maps: OS Explorer 110 (Torquay & Dawlish)

Path description: Road and footpath

Start point: Pedestrian access to car park (GR SX 868795)

Parking: Chudleigh Town Hall, Market Way, Chudleigh, TQ13 0HL

Dog Friendly: Keep on a lead on the road and near livestock. Dogs are not allowed in the Chudleigh Rocks Gardens

Public toilets: In Chudleigh Car Park

Nearest food: Café at Chudleigh Rocks, pubs and cafes in Chudleigh

1. Begin at Chudleigh Car Park and walk past the library to the footpath which leads to the main street. Turn left and walk down the road. This is the main shopping area and also has a number of cafés and galleries. At Clifford Street turn right and walk down the footpath. This leads past houses and emerges at a road junction. Cross the road and go over a bridge. Just after the bridge is a footpath on the right by Garden Spot Lane.

2. Walk down this path until you reach a footpath on the left. Go through the gate. Walk a short way up this field pathway to another gate on the right.

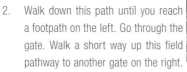

   Go through this gate. From the gate walk along the path which opens out into a field. Go through a large gate. Walk towards the trees and take the track up towards the wooded area. Traces of the Iron Age hill fort and settlement can be seen around here with some good views of Chudleigh. Take the path that veers to the left through woodland towards a gate. Go through the gate onto the road.

3. At the road junction turn right and continue walking with the walls of Ugbrooke Park on the left. Ugbrooke Park is a stately home which features designs by Capability Brown and Robert Adam and is open periodically to the public. Continue along the road until reaching a junction.

4. At the junction take the road to the right which goes downhill. This route has some good views of Dartmoor to the left. Take the footpath to the right through a gate. Go through a second gate. This leads across a field. Follow the path through it and around to the left behind a large house to a gate in the corner of the field. Go through the gate and cross a stream. On the left is a path leading up through trees to the road.

5. At the road junction cross over to the pavement and continue walking to the right. Chudleigh Rocks is on the right-hand side and makes an interesting break. Continue walking along this road past the church and shops to the car park where the walk began.

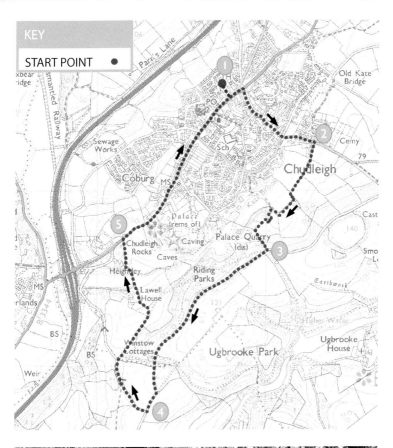

COLYTON

This walk begins in the historic town of Colyton and leads through beautiful countryside to the wetlands of the River Axe and the hamlet of Colyford. It includes an optional ride on a narrow-gauge heritage tram to neighbouring Seaton.

Colyton was once called the most rebellious town in Devon due to the number of local residents who joined the Monmouth Rebellion in 1685. Over 100 men joined the ill-fated uprising against King James II when the Duke of Monmouth landed at Lyme Regis. As a consequence many local men were hanged and others were transported to the West Indies. This is a medieval town with a lot of history and the maze of Saxon-style streets are a delight to explore. The town marks the border between the Durotriges tribe from Dorset and the Dumnonii of Devon and this may explain why there are several Iron Age hill forts in the area.

Colyton Grammar School has been in existence since 1546 and was founded by twenty feoffees (trustees) from Colyton who purchased land for the good of the town. Today the school lies in the neighbouring hamlet of Colyford. The Seaton Electric Tramway runs across the road in Colyford on its route between Colyton and Seaton. Narrow-gauge heritage trams are a unique way of travelling through two nature reserves to the sea. They traverse what was once the London and South West Railway route and is now a popular visitor attraction. The nature reserves are popular habitats for terns, kingfishers and many more wading birds.

THE BASICS

Distance: 3½ miles / 5.6km

Gradient: Mainly flat

Severity: Easy

Approx. time to walk: 2–3 hours

Stiles: None, but four kissing gates

Maps: OS Explorer 116 (Lyme Regis & Bridport)

Path description: Road and footpaths

Start point: Entrance to Seaton Tramway car park (GR SY 251941)

Parking: Seaton Tramway Car Park, Cownhayne Lane (EX24 6HA)

Dog Friendly: Keep on a lead on the road and around livestock

Public toilets: In Colyton town centre and at the Tramway termini

Nearest food: Colyton Tramway Station has a tea room; cafés in Colyton and Seaton

1. Park at Colyton Tramway Car Park. Walk back out of the car park to the exit. Continue walking along the road to the junction ahead. Turn left and walk over the bridge to Colyton. Walk along Dolphin Street to the centre of town. You will pass a second car park which is another potential starting point for this walk.

2. Walk towards the Market Square. The town hall is on the right. At the road junction turn left and then take the road on the right that leads uphill.

3. Walk up the hill, which has beautiful views to the left. As the road levels out there is a picnic spot and viewing point on the left-hand side. *Dogs are not permitted in this viewing area*. Continue along the road. On the right is an old tombstone placed there in 1807. This is the Doctor's Stone and was set up by Revd Dr F. Barnes, the vicar of Colyton from 1807 to 1860, as his favourite viewpoint. Just a little further up the road on the right is a footpath beside a house.

4. Go through the kissing gate past some stables. Continue through another kissing gate to a third gate. Go through this gate towards the road but take a sharp left turn just before the road to a narrow lane.

5. Go down this lane, which runs alongside Colyton School. At the junction with the road turn left. Walk down the road to another junction and cross that road. Walk down this road to a junction with a busy road and turn left.

6. Continue with care along this busy road which leads to Colyford. Walk past St Gregory's Church on the left. On the right are some old petrol pumps which were once part of a motor museum.

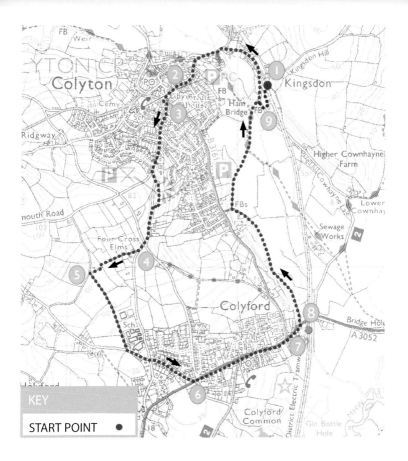

KEY

START POINT ●

7. Continue past the Wheelwright's Arms. On the left just past a road junction is a footpath. At this point there is an option to catch the electric tram to Seaton or alternatively to return to Colyton.

8. Take the footpath on the left-hand side. This leads along the riverside and through a meadow. Continue walking ahead on the marked trail. Walk under a pipe that is raised above the trail. Walk past a footbridge and head towards the footpath in the top left corner of the field.

9. Take this path and walk a short distance to a road junction. Turn sharp right and walk up the road to the tram station on the left.

    After the walk there is an option of taking a walking tour through the streets of Colyton or catching the electric tram to Seaton.

DARTINGTON

THIS WALK EXPLORES THE BEAUTIFUL DARTINGTON ESTATE AND TAKES IN HISTORIC STAVERTON BRIDGE BEFORE RETURNING VIA A RIVERSIDE WALK. THERE IS AN OPTION TO ENJOY A STEAM TRAIN TRIP ON THE ICONIC SOUTH DEVON RAILWAY WHICH RUNS BETWEEN BUCKFASTLEIGH AND TOTNES WITH A STOP IN STAVERTON.

The Dartington Hall site is steeped in history, dating back to the 14th century when Richard II gave it to his half-brother John Holand in 1384. Even before that there is evidence of a Roman occupation and mention in an AD 833 Royal Charter. In Norman times Dartington was held by William De Falaise from Normandy. In the 15th century Dartington became a great house and garden under generations of the Holand family and in 1487 the land passed back to the Crown. For a time Dartington was owned by two of Henry VIII's wives; Catherine Howard and Catherine Parr. The Champernowne family purchased Dartington in 1559 and retained the property for 300 years. During the agricultural depression of the 19th century they were forced to sell most of the land. Today Dartington Hall is a charity that works with activists, artists and entrepreneurs worldwide. The grounds are open to the public to walk in.

Staverton Bridge was built around 1413 and crosses the River Dart. It is one of the finest surviving medieval bridges in Devon and has an interesting past. Staverton Bridge has been the haunt of a highwayman, the site of a murder, and has even given its name to a professional folk group. Today it is possible to see kingfishers from the bridge and cross to the South Devon Railway or explore the pretty village of Staverton.

THE BASICS

Distance: 4 miles / 6.4km

Gradient: Undulating but mainly flat

Severity: An easy walk but there are some steep steps around the river section

Approx. time to walk: 3 hours

Stiles: None

Maps: OS Explorer 110 (Torquay & Dawlish)

Path description: Tarmacked road, footpaths

Start point: Visitor Centre at Dartington Hall (GR SX 799628)

Parking: Main car park, Dartington Hall (TQ9 6EP)

Dog Friendly: Keep on a lead near livestock, on the roads, and near the railways

Public toilets: Dartington Hall

Nearest food: White Hart Pub or Roundhouse Café, Dartington Hall; Sea Trout Inn at Staverton

1. The walk starts by the visitor centre at Dartington Hall. Walk down Park Road, which is just below the visitor centre entrance. At the junction take the road to the left marked Warren Road. Follow the wooded road.

2. At the end of the road take the footpath to the left. Go through the gate and continue walking along a path with the estate wall on your right. Go through a second gate. After the path curves round to the right there is a fork. Take the left-hand path.

3. Continue through a gate and onto the path that leads ahead through the trees. This is a beautiful pine forest with some deciduous trees. Continue walking along the woodland path until there are steps on the right.

4. If you plan to return to Dartington at this point take the steps and follow the instructions from step 6. Alternatively, if you plan to continue to Staverton Bridge then take the path ahead through the trees.

5. After a short while you will arrive at a junction with two paths. Take the right-hand path and walk towards the gate. Go through the gate and onto the road. Turn sharp right and walk around the road to Staverton Bridge. There are some beautiful views across the River Dart. Just ahead is Staverton Station, where steam trains run to Totnes and Buckfastleigh. Retrace your steps back over the bridge and through the footpaths and woods to the steps which will now be on your left.

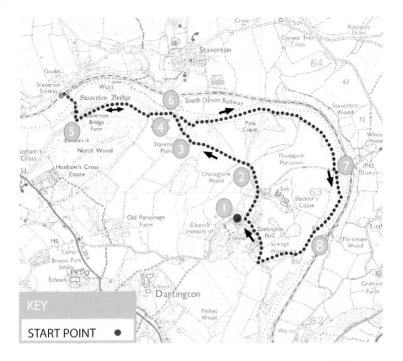

6. Walk down the steps towards the river and continue on the marked trail. The steps descend steeply at first and go up and down along this path through woodland which leads around to the right as it follows the river. Eventually this path emerges on a footpath beside the river. Continue on this path with a wooded area to your right and the river on your left. You may be able to hear the steam train and see it on sections of this path as the track runs on the other side of the river.

7. Cross a stile and keep walking on the riverside path. Cross another stile. Walk past a small building and continue following the riverside path.

8. Look out for a kissing gate, on the right, behind a hedge. This leads to a path, between shrubbery and a field boundary, which opens out into a field. Turn left. At the next gate, cross the field to the road back to Dartington Hall.

After the walk you may like to explore the gardens at Dartington or browse the shops at Dartington which are a short distance away.

DITTISHAM

This walk starts from The Ham Car Park and heads through the upper village with views of the River Dart. It heads out over fields and returns into Dittisham.

If this name appears familiar then perhaps a character from *Five Little Pigs* might give a clue. Agatha Christie named Lady Dittisham after the village opposite her summer residence at Greenway. Even today visitors can relive the first pages of Agatha Christie's *Ordeal By Innocence* by ringing the large bell to summon a ferry across the River Dart. The river taxis run daily between Greenway and Dittisham; a popular activity for visitors. The Greenway boathouse at the landing was Agatha Christie's setting for the murder in *Dead Man's Folly*. In the middle of the river lies the Scold Stone or Anchor Stone. In medieval times unfaithful wives were tied to this by the menfolk of Dittisham as a punishment.

Dittisham, or Ditsum to the locals, is a quaint village with sweeping views of the Dart Estuary, charming cottages and narrow lanes. There are plum orchards where the famous Dittisham plums are grown, and footpaths meandering across rolling countryside. The village is located at the widest part of the Dart, and The Ham is the area where people walk dogs or relax and look out at the river. This is one of the most picturesque villages on the Dart Estuary and walking around here is exceptionally beautiful.

THE BASICS

Distance: 3 miles / 4.8km (not including optional trip to Greenway House)

Gradient: Two steep hills but otherwise fairly flat

Severity: Easy

Approx. time to walk: 2 hours

Stiles: None

Maps: OS Explorer OL20 (South Devon)

Path description: Road, fields and footpaths

Start point: Ham Lane Car Park, Dittisham (GR SX 865551)

Parking: Ham Lane Car Park, Dittisham (TQ6 0HS)

Dog Friendly: Keep on leads near livestock and on the road

Public toilets: Ham Lane Car Park, Dittisham

Nearest food: Anchorstone Café, Dittisham (it is advisable to book at weekends)

DITTISHAM WALK

1. From The Ham Car Park walk back out uphill towards the road. Continue walking through the village and past St George's Church. This dates from the 14th century.

2. Follow the road around to the right where there are lovely views of the River Dart. This road narrows. Just a short distance up the hill is a footpath on the left. Go through the kissing gate and walk across the field. There are splendid river views on the right. Go through a second field and walk downhill across it to the gap in the lower right corner.

3. The footpath emerges at a bend in a road. Immediately to the left take the 'untarmacked track'. Walk up this track, which is steep in parts, to the main road. During spring and summer the path is full of wild flowers. At the road turn left. Around 50 yards on the right is a footpath. Go through the gate and walk across this field to a footpath sign. Walkers will once again be rewarded with beautiful views of the River Dart.

4. At the footpath sign take the path to the left. Follow this downhill. At the junction take the next right and walk down the road into Dittisham. From here walk across the beach at low tide or take the path to the car park and the start of the walk. Alternatively get something to eat at the local pub or café. On the wall by the slipway is the famous bell where you can give a loud ring to summon the ferry to Greenway.

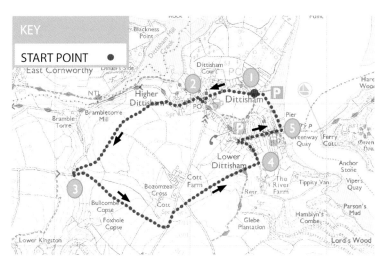

GREAT TORRINGTON

T<small>HIS WALK STARTS FROM THE TOWN AND HEADS OUT
PAST MEDIEVAL STRIP LYNCHETS TO AN OLD LEPER COLONY
BEFORE CONTINUING ALONG THE</small> R<small>IVER</small> T<small>ORRIDGE AND
WOODLAND. IT RETURNS TO THE TOWN VIA VIEWPOINTS OF
THE SURROUNDING COUNTRYSIDE AND THE</small> D<small>ARTINGTON</small>
G<small>LASS</small> F<small>ACTORY.</small>

Great Torrington sits on an inland clifftop on the River Torridge. The surrounding area
was the inspiration for Henry Williamson's book *Tarka the Otter*, written in the 1920s.
Great Torrington is also renowned for the part it played in the English Civil War in bringing
about the demise of the Royalist army. On 16 February 1646 the Battle of Torrington took
place when 17,000 men fought in the streets of the town. During the battle a stray spark
ignited the church where the Royalists had stored munitions and an explosion of eighty
barrels of gunpowder killed many Royalist soldiers as well as Parliamentarian prisoners.
The explosion effectively ended the battle and Royalist commander Lord Hopton escaped
to Cornwall, where he eventually surrendered.

The Battle of Torrington ended any resistance in the West Country and eventually led to
the execution of Charles I. Each year Great Torrington marks the anniversary of the battle
with a torchlit procession. During the 12th century the ground known as The Common
was given to the people of Torrington and the rights to the land were transferred to a
conservation committee in 1889. Today there are over 20 miles of footpaths that can be
used by the public around the town.

THE BASICS

Distance: 4 miles / 6.4km

Gradient: Undulating

Severity: Easy

Approx. time to walk: 2–3 hours

Stiles: Three

Maps: OS Explorer 139 (Bideford, Ilfracombe & Barnstaple)

Path description: Roads and footpaths

Start point: Barley Grove, Castle Street, Torrington (GR SS 496189)

Parking: Barley Grove, Castle Street, Torrington (EX38 8EZ)

Dog Friendly: Keep on a lead near traffic and the fast-flowing river. Dogs are not permitted at the Dartington Glass Factory

Public toilets: Pannier Market, Torrington; Dartington Glass Factory

Nearest food: Several places in Torrington. En route Torrington Cycle Hire near Puffing Billy sells coffees, and Dartington Glass Factory serves snacks

GREAT TORRINGTON WALK

1. Walk from the Pannier Market Car Park down the slope path to the viewpoint on Great Torrington Common. Take the path to the right marked Millennium Path. This leads downhill and to the left are views of the narrow fields once worked by lepers. These are the two narrow strips of land. Continue down the path to Taddiport Bridge.

2. Take some time to cross the bridge and walk into the hamlet of Taddiport. This was where the medieval leper colony was housed until it fell into disuse during the 17th century. There is a leper burial site and cottages with names relating to its past as a colony for people with this disease.

3. Head back across the bridge and take the footpath on the left along the river. Walk past the disused Dairy Crest Factory. Cross a stile and then a second stile. The river is fast flowing at this point and walkers with young children or dogs will need to be careful. Cross a third stile. At a junction in the path with a works site, turn right. At the top of this path turn left onto the Rolle Road which was used to transport limestone and clay in the early 19th century. This was abandoned in 1871 in favour of the railways. Continue along a wooded path with views over the River Torridge. This leads to a road underpass to the Puffing Billy, which was the terminus of the London and South West Railways. There is also a cycle shop where a leisurely tea or coffee may be purchased.

4. At the Puffing Billy side of the bridge walk up the road to a footpath sign on the left. Follow this path to Alexander's Path on the right. Follow this trail ahead through woodland. It goes uphill and emerges at a small car park. Take the path to the left.

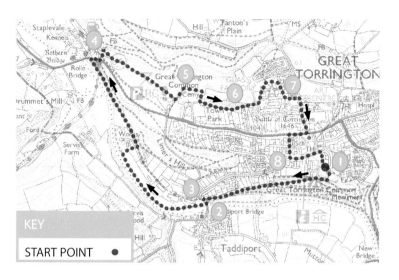

KEY

START POINT ●

5. Walk along this path to the end of the wall and then turn right. Continue along this path, which borders the town cemetery. At the end of this wall turn right again. The path forks – take the left fork.

6. Slightly to the left is a path leading to the Dartington Glass Factory and Showroom where there are tours and also snacks.

7. Walk uphill and out of the factory entrance and turn left down Linden Close. Turn right and walk towards the church. At the junction turn right. Take the first left down Whites Lane. The old glove factory is on the right.

8. At the bottom of this road turn left. Walk through the centre of town and through the pannier market to the car park and the end of the walk.

Hartland Point

HARTLAND

This walk starts from Hartland Quay and takes the South West Coast Footpath to Blegberry Beach before heading inland to Hartland Abbey. Returning via Stoke the walk ends back at Hartland Quay.

Descending the steep hill to Hartland Quay visitors are frequently captivated by the dramatic cliff scenery that awaits them. Hartland is strikingly beautiful and an Area of Outstanding Natural Beauty but has an exposed coastline with unpredictable weather and blustery winds. With soaring granite cliffs the Hartland Peninsula is one of the most isolated parts of Devon and faces the Atlantic. There are sheltered valleys here too and waterfalls tumbling through the countryside. In the past this has been the haunt of smugglers and pirates. At one time pirates occupied nearby Lundy Island and there were periodic raids on the mainland. Hartland Quay was once a busy port wedged between the cliffs and was destroyed by the power of the sea a century ago. The warehouses and customs houses have now been converted into a hotel which provides a warm welcome after a bracing walk across the cliffs. The museum here tells the history of the local smuggling trade and the many shipwrecks off the coast.

Hartland Abbey dates from the 12th century and housed monks from nearby St Nectan's Church. After the Dissolution of the Monasteries Henry VIII gave Hartland Abbey to William Abbot, his head butler. The house passed through his descendants to Sir Hugh Stucley and is now open to the public along with the beautiful gardens.

THE BASICS

Distance: 5 miles / 8km

Gradient: Some steep ascents on the cliff path

Severity: Some steep parts but otherwise an easy walk

Approx. time to walk: 3 hours

Stiles: Four

Maps: OS Explorer 126 (Clovelly & Hartland)

Path description: Coastal footpath, road and lanes

Start point: Car park just above Hartland Quay Hotel (GR SS 224248)

Parking: Car park at Hartland Quay Hotel, Hartland (EX39 6DU)

Dog Friendly: Keep on a lead near livestock and the road

Public toilets: On Hartland Quay next to hotel and at St Nectan's Church in Stoke

Nearest food: Wreckers Bar at Hartland Quay Hotel. Hartland Abbey Gardens are open periodically and it is advisable to check the opening times if you plan to visit (www.hartlandabbey.com)

1. From Hartland Quay Hotel Car Park walk back up the road and take the coastal footpath on the left. This is on the left side of the upper car park. This path leads steeply upwards via steps carved into the cliff. There are spectacular views of the coast from this path. The path emerges at Rocket House.

2. Rocket House was built during the 1890s and stored rocket-launching equipment for the Hartland Quay Lifesaving Apparatus Company. Take the footpath to the side of Rocket House and walk towards the stone

Pleasure House Folly in the field. This is a well-known landmark on Hartland and is believed to have been an old warrener's house that was later re-fashioned into a Victorian folly. Continue on the path ahead which leads to Dyer's Lookout. Follow the path around to the right, which leads through a gate and over a small footbridge named Blackpool Mill Bridge. Ahead is a path. Take this and follow it round to the left. This leads past a cottage and ahead is Blackpool Mill Beach.

3. On the right is a steep uphill track. Walk up this path, which leads to a stile. Cross this stile for views of Blegberry Beach and waterfall. At a second stile take the path to the right before the stile. Follow this path past fields to a gate onto a lane.

4. Go through the gate past some caravans to the end of the lane. At the end of this lane turn right.

5. Continue down the road and past the buildings in the hamlet of Berry. Just past Berry House about 50 yards up the road there is a footpath sign on the left.

6. Take this footpath, which leads through three fields. There are beautiful views across the valley. At the end of the third field go through the gate in the bottom right corner. This leads onto a narrow road.

7. Walk down the road, which twists round and emerges at Hartland Abbey Gardens. There are bluebells along this route in springtime.

8. Cross the bridge and take the road to the right towards Stoke. The road goes uphill and levels out at Stoke village. Walk towards St Nectan's Church, which is known as the Cathedral of North Devon because of its size.

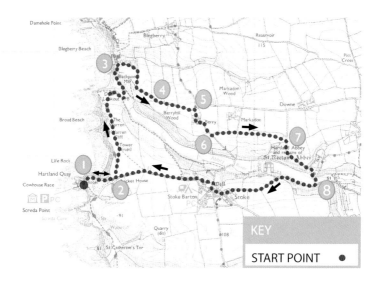

KEY

START POINT ●

9. At the church take the small lane to the right. Just a few yards up the lane on the left-hand side are some steps and a stone stile leading through the church yard. Cross the next stile and follow a small lane ahead. This leads past houses and is a track that avoids walking on the busy road. Follow the footpath across drives and past several small stiles. Eventually this emerges into an open field with a view of the Pleasure House Folly ahead.

10. Continue down this path towards the house on the left. This is the Rocket House. This path emerges onto the road and continues back down to Hartland Quay with sweeping views of the coastline. At Hartland Quay, enjoy a drink in the Wreckers Bar and learn about smuggling in the small museum.

HEMBURY WOODS

THIS WALK EXPLORES HEMBURY WOODS NEAR BUCKFAST AND INCLUDES WOODLAND PATHS, AN IRON AGE HILL FORT, AND AN OPTIONAL VISIT TO BUCKFAST ABBEY AFTERWARDS.

Hembury Woods is just outside Buckfast on the edge of Dartmoor. In prehistoric times Hembury Castle commanded magnificent views across the Devon countryside and is 135 metres (450 feet) above sea level. Surveys of the fort indicate it had a single entrance and an inner and outer rampart surrounded by a ditch. It is believed to have been a trading and storage centre for minerals as traces of tin have been found during excavations. The River Dart traverses these woods, adding to the significance of this fort in ancient times. During Norman times a thousand years later the site is reputed to have been a motte and bailey castle. In the woods there are silver birch, oak, hazel, and holly amongst other trees.

Buckfast Abbey is close to Hembury Woods and has been a religious site for almost a thousand years. It was originally founded during the reign of Canute in 1018, and closed by Henry VIII during the Dissolution of the Monasteries. The site was bought by a group

of French Benedictine monks in 1882. Construction of a new abbey church started in 1907, with never more than six monks working on the project at any one time. The abbey is known for its beekeeping and tonic wine production. Today there is still a Benedictine monastic community here and a successful conference and visitor centre.

THE BASICS

Distance: 2 miles / 3.2km

Gradient: A steep ascent at the beginning and a descent during the walk; otherwise undulating

Severity: This is a fairly easy walk. However, it is easy to become disorientated in woodland, especially as ongoing woodland management can cause temporary tracks to appear and disappear. It is important to take a map and compass when walking in unfamiliar woodland.

Approx. time to walk: 1–2 hours

Stiles: One

Maps: OS Explorer OL28 (Dartmoor)

Path description: Road; woodland path which can be muddy in parts

Start point: Hembury Woods Car Park (GR SX 730680)

Parking: Hembury Woods Car Park, Hembury Cock Hill, Buckfast (TQ11 0HN)

Dog Friendly: This is a popular spot for dog walking, but keep them on a lead where sheep are grazing in the open areas of the hill fort

Public toilets: None in the woods but there are some at Buckfast Abbey nearby

Nearest food: Buckfast Abbey restaurant

HEMBURY WOODS WALK

1. Walk out of the car park to the road and go uphill. This road is steep and eventually levels slightly.

2. Look for a stile on the right-hand side. Take this stile and walk ahead to the hill fort. There are still traces of the raised parts of the fort here but today this is mainly open grassland with trees. Walk towards some trees ahead and then take the track to the left.

3. This is a well-defined path leading to the left and to a gate. Go through this gate and walk straight ahead. After a short distance there is a car park on the left. Just ahead of this is a fork in the paths. Take the grassy right-hand path that leads downhill. This would have been the base of the hill fort. The path leads to the ruined Hembury Barn.

4. Continue past this building to a fork in the paths marked by a post. Take the path that leads straight ahead and slightly to the right. At the next fork in the paths take the central path. This emerges into a small clearing with a gate to the left.

5. Go through the gate and follow the track steeply downhill. This may be slippery in wet weather. In spring these woods are covered in bluebells. At the end of the path there is a stone wall. Take the path to the right. Continue along this path, walking straight ahead.

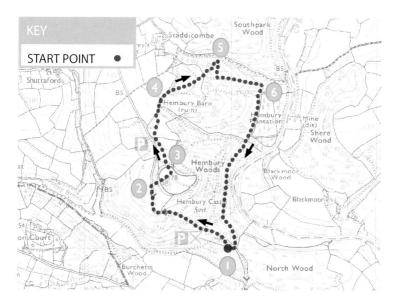

6.   Continue along the wooded track, which emerges onto a wider and more defined path with markers. These posts point ahead to the car park and to the fort. Keep walking straight ahead following the car park signs. Eventually this walk ends at the cark park where it began. After the walk a visit to Buckfast Abbey is an option.

LEE

THIS WALK EXPLORES THE SMALL VILLAGE OF LEE AND HEADS UP WINDCUTTER HILL WITH VIEWS OF THE COAST BEFORE HEADING BACK VIA BOROUGH VALLEY.

Lee is a village near Woolacombe on the North Devon Coast. The centre of the village is around a quarter of a mile from the sea and has a pub and shop. At low tide there are lots of rock pools on the shore with a path to Sandy Cove. St Matthew's Church was built in 1835 and has 16th-century woodcarvings inside. There are also good examples of traditional stencilled wall coverings. Beside the village hall is a Pixie Meadow, now used as a play area and for local fairs and events. Lee Bay was a notorious smuggling

centre in the 19th century. One of the most infamous smugglers in the area was Hannibal Richards, who was a member of Cruel Coppinger's gang. Together with his wife he used the footpaths around this village to spirit away the illicit cargoes of brandy and tobacco landed here. The coastline is lined with rocks and many a ship has been wrecked on the shoreline around here.

During the 1970s the hills around Lee were planted with Sitka spruce pine trees. These are salt resistant and are more resilient in the sea air and the relentless westerly winds. On the landscape around Windcutter Hill are several wooded areas with trees which have grown at extreme angles due to the ferocity of the prevailing winds. The area around Borough Woods has survived as ancient woodland because the land was too steep to cultivate. However, many oak trees were felled during World War I. Today there are several species here including ash, hazel and rhododendron. Lee is known for the Old Maid's Cottage just downhill from the village hall. This inspired the poem, 'Three Old Maids from Lee', which is based on the tale of local women who were too picky about their suitors.

THE BASICS

Distance: 2 miles / 3.2km

Gradient: A steep ascent and descent

Severity: There are steep parts to this walk but footpaths are marked

Approx. time to walk: 1–2 hours

Stiles: Two

Maps: OS Explorer 139 (Bideford, Ilfracombe & Barnstaple)

Path description: There are steep ascents and descents on this walk. The footpaths through the woods are marked but do stay on the identified trails

Start point: By the village hall (GR SS 485463)

Parking: Village Hall car park opposite the church (EX34 8LW)

Dog Friendly: Must be kept on a lead near livestock and on the road

Public toilets: Signposted near the Grampus Inn in Lee Village

Nearest food: Grampus Inn in Lee Bay

LEE WALK

1. Walk out of the village hall car park. Ahead is St Matthew's Church and the old schoolroom which is now a shop. The bell on the schoolroom roof comes from a shipwreck that occurred here in 1858. Turn left and follow the footpath on the left. The path is then signposted to the right. Continue walking uphill through woodland. The path winds upwards quite steeply and finishes at a gate leading to a field. Go through the gate and cross the field. Look behind you for good views of the area. Continue ahead to a stile and cross this, continuing over the field. This is Windcutter Hill.

2. At a signpost pointing in three directions take the footpath to the right marked Borough Valley. Walk along this footpath to a stile leading to an open field with marshy areas. Walk ahead, keeping to the left and the fence as much as possible, heading in the direction of the forest. The ground is very uneven with raised edges in this field. In the bottom left-hand corner of the field is a footpath marker and gate leading to Borough Woods.

3. Follow the marked footpath through the trees. This leads steeply downhill. Continue walking on the trail until it emerges at a junction with an unmarked path. Cross this path and follow the marked footpath steeply downhill through the forest. This leads to the right, indicated by the yellow marker on the tree, and curves around and downhill, emerging at a clearing. Take the path ahead which leads over a footbridge to a wooded path.

4. Continue walking along this path with the stream on the right. Go through a kissing gate and continue on the path in Borough Woods. At a footbridge cross this and go through the kissing gate. This leads into an open field. Walk across this to the footpath and turn right. Continue up the road past cottages and the Grampus Inn. At the end of the road turn right. Walk up the hill passing the Old Maids Cottage on the left and return to the car park where the walk began.

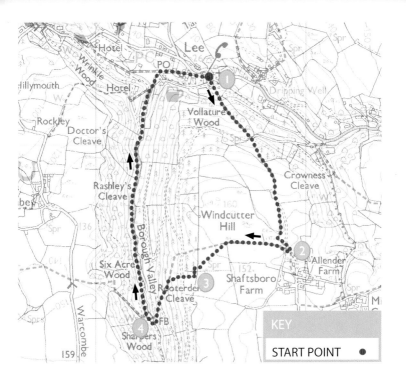

KEY

START POINT ●

This walk heads past Otterton Mill and runs along the River Otter and salt marshes and crosses the river to return to the village. There is an alternate walk of 1 mile (1.5km) by crossing the Clamour Bridge part of the way through this walk.

There has been a mill at Otterton for over a thousand years. William the Conqueror gave the lands to the Abbots of St Michel of Normandy and the mill is listed in the Domesday Book. Otterton Mill was one of the most powerful mills in Devon and was run by the French for 400 years until Henry V gave it to the nuns at Syon Abbey. Following the Dissolution of the Monasteries Otterton Mill was given to Richard Duke by Henry VIII and it remained with this family for 200 years. In 1785 it passed to Dennis Rolle, who married into the Clinton family. Today Otterton Mill is part of the Clinton Devon Estate and is the most powerful watermill in Devon. Milling is done every two weeks by a team of volunteers who produce high-quality flour. Visitors can watch the process and see the waterwheels and millstones in action. Otterton Mill is also a craft centre with a café and deli selling locally milled flour. Milling times are listed on the mill website (www.ottertonmill.com).

The River Otter at Otterton is a habitat for many wild animals including beavers, kingfishers and otters. Wading birds can be spotted around the salt marshes and riverbeds in this area. South of the White Bridge is a Site of Special Scientific Interest and important nature reserve. There are lots of birding hides there and opportunities to spot warblers, wading birds and even grebes. At Otterton Mill there is a board where visitors can list the animals seen on a walk in the area.

THE BASICS

Distance: 3 miles / 4.8km

Gradient: Mostly level with one short uphill section

Severity: Easy

Approx. time to walk: 2 hours

Stiles: None

Maps: OS Explorer 115 (Exmouth & Sidmouth)

Path description: Mainly footpaths with some road walking

Start point: Short walk to Otterton Mill off Fore Street (GR SY 079853)

Parking: Near Otterton Mill (EX9 7HG). Try Roper's Lane (EX9 7JF). Otterton Mill has limited parking which they prefer to reserve for customers

Dog Friendly: Keep on a lead near livestock and on the main road

Public toilets: No public toilets in the village. Toilets for customers are available at Otterton Mill

Nearest food: At Otterton Mill

1. The walk starts at Otterton Mill. Walk past the mill to go over the bridge.

2. Take the footpath marked on the left and walk down the steps to the footpath. Continue along this path past fields and the river bank.

3. At the Clamour Bridge continue walking along the path. The Clamour Bridge is thought to be named after an old stone bridge that once stood here; the Devon dialect for these structures was *clammer*. If you plan to do the short walk cross the bridge, climb the steps at the opposite end and turn left to head back to Otterton, following the walk instructions from step 6.

4. You will pass a small aqueduct on the right. Ahead are the salt marshes where there are lots of birds and walkers may spot kingfishers or other species. Until the 15th century this river was navigable. Salt had been extracted from here since Roman times and was a major industry during the middle ages.

5. At the White Bridge cross over and turn left towards Otterton. Walk up this path where there are views across to the River Otter on the left. This path leads uphill and then levels out.

6. Beside two pillars are steps leading down to the Clamour Bridge. Take the path that leads through the two pillars and is a permissive route. Follow this woodland trail which leads back into the village. At the end of the road turn left.

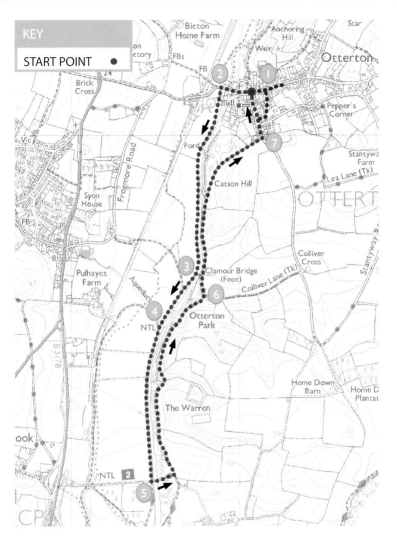

KEY

START POINT ●

7. Follow the road back through the village. There are lots of cob and thatch cottages in Otterton and the Church of St Michael and All Angels is an impressive building built in the 1870s. It stands on the site of a Saxon church and a Benedictine monastery. The road leads back to the mill and the start of the walk. Don't forget to list any bird or animal species spotted on the walk on the board back at Otterton Mill.

PLYMOUTH

This is a short walk packed with history and heads off from near Plymouth Hoe with views across the Sound. It continues along the seafront and passes the old Millbay Docks area before returning inland to the Barbican via the Plymouth Gin Distillery and the Mayflower Steps.

Plymouth is steeped in naval and maritime history and there are reminders everywhere of the heritage in this city. Plymouth Sound is one of the finest natural harbours in the world and has seen many momentous events. This is where Sir Francis Drake famously played bowls whilst awaiting the Spanish Armada in 1588, and he is now immortalised with a statue on Plymouth Hoe. The impressive Citadel dominating the Hoe was built in the 17th century and acted as a defence to the waterways off Plymouth. Close by are poignant memorials to those lost at sea in various conflicts. The Barbican is one of the oldest parts of Plymouth and is full of historic pubs once frequented by press gangs and seafarers. In modern times eclectic shops and art galleries have moved in. In 1620 it was the departure point for the Pilgrim Fathers who set sail for America in the *Mayflower*.

Plymouth Gin was founded in 1793 after Nelson's naval officers developed a taste for the drink in place of rum. No ship left port without a good supply of gin. Today Plymouth Gin is still made at navy strength or 57 per cent alcohol by volume (ABV) and 100 per cent English proof. Traditionally gin was stored with gunpowder on ships. If navy strength gin was spilled the gunpowder would still ignite.

THE BASICS

Distance: 2 miles / 3.2km

Gradient: Mainly flat

Severity: An easy walk

Approx. time to walk: 1–2 hours

Stiles: None

Maps: OS Explorer 108 (Lower Tamar Valley & Plymouth)

Path description: Pavements. There is an admission charge to tour the Plymouth Gin Distillery, which must be pre-booked. There is a small display in the shop which is free (www.plymouthgin.com)

Start point: Entrance to Elphinstone car park (GR SX 483538)

Parking: Elphinstone Car Park, off Madeira Road, Plymouth (PL1 2NU)

Dog Friendly: Dogs must be kept on a lead on the road and are not allowed in the gin distillery

Public toilets: Elphinstone car park

Nearest food: Lots of bars and cafés on the walk in Plymouth

PLYMOUTH WALK

1. Walk out of the Elphinstone Car Park and turn left. On the left is the area known as Barbican Wharves and a prominent part of the Plymouth Waterfront. The imposing building on the right is the Royal Citadel, which was designed during the reign of Charles II and protected Plymouth from seaward approaches. Continue along the road to a pair of cannon on the left. These date from 1811 and 1819. On the other side of the road is the Royal Marines Memorial.

2. A few yards along the road and looking out onto Plymouth Sound is the art deco Tinside Lido. This was built in 1935 and is still used during the summer months. Take some time to explore Plymouth Hoe, which has the iconic Smeaton's Tower (a former Eddystone lighthouse) and statues of famous seafarers including Sir Francis Drake, and is an open green area. Just below Plymouth Hoe is the Memorial Garden with plaques commemorating various conflicts from the Falklands to Korea. Continue walking along the road, following it round to West Hoe and with views out to sea and Drake's Island.

3. At the junction with Grand Parade take the small path to the left nearest the sea front. Along the wall of this passage are models of ships and submarines that are based in Plymouth. These include HMS *Ocean* and HMS *Orkney*. At the end of this path take the road ahead (Great Western Road) which passes the site of the old Millbay Docks. On the walls are historic signs which were once part of the dockyard. Continue walking up the road with Millbay Park on your right.

4. At the roundabout cross the road towards Millbay Park and then continue along to the second exit and Millbay Road which becomes the Crescent. Turn right and walk down this road to Notte Street. On the right hand side is the anchor from HMS *Ark Royal*. When the ship was decommissioned in 1979 one of the anchors was given to her home base in Plymouth.

5. Continue walking down Notte Street until you reach Southside Street on the right. Walk down this road and a few yards down on the right is Plymouth Gin at the Blackfriars Distillery. Gin has been distilled here since the late 17th century and it is a famous product of the city. Continue walking down Southside Street into the Barbican. There are old shipping buildings, customs houses and historic pubs

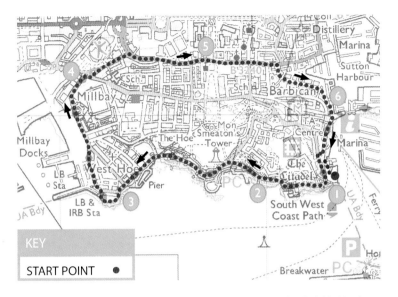

within a very short distance and a maze of small streets. The Dolphin Hotel was the setting for some of the artist Beryl Cook's paintings. The Minerva Inn on Looe Street was the haunt of the press gangs and is the oldest pub in Plymouth.

6. From the bottom of Southside Street follow the sea front around past the shops and boats. Ahead are the Mayflower Steps where 100 puritans set sail for America in 1620. Walk from the Mayflower Steps back up the hill where there is a memorial to local fishermen and seafarers on the right. Just a few yards up is the car park where the walk began. Plymouth has lots of options at the end of this walk, from visiting the shopping centres to spending time in the Mayflower Museum or taking a boat trip down the River Tamar.

Plymouth Gin Distillery

Barbican - Mark Tremain

SALCOMBE

This walk follows the beautiful coastal path around Salcombe and includes an optional visit to the museum and gardens at Overbeck's before returning to the beaches. It passes hidden coves and the sites of shipwrecks, and there are spellbinding viewpoints along the trail.

Salcombe is a beautiful coastal town in the South Hams district of Devon on the Kingsbridge Estuary. It is renowned for its historic shipbuilding history and for the shellfish trade. During the 19th century Salcombe was a centre for fruit trading, with boats sailing to the Azores and Caribbean and bringing back oranges, lemons, pineapples and more. Salcombe Schooners were designed to be sailed with few hands on board. Just off the coast of Salcombe are many shipwrecks. In Starehole Bay lies the Finnish windjammer **Herzogin Cecilie**, which sank in Soar Mill Cove in 1936. In 1916 thirteen of the fifteen-man crew of the local lifeboat, the **William and Emma**, were lost on the infamous Salcombe Bar. In Salcombe Museum the Wreck Room depicts these and other shipwrecks from this stretch of coastline.

Overbeck's is an Edwardian house and now a quirky museum filled with the inventions of Otto Overbeck, a scientist and inventor who lived here. In World War I it was a convalescent hospital for wounded soldiers. Displays include a musical polyphon and the famous rejuvenator. There are also beautiful sub-tropical gardens to explore at this National Trust property.

iStock

THE BASICS

Distance: 4 miles / 6.4km

Gradient: Quite hilly in parts

Severity: A pleasant walk in good weather but may be slippery if wet and/or windy

Approx. time to walk: 2–3 hours

Stiles: Four kissing gates

Maps: OS Explorer OL20 (South Devon)

Path description: Road, coastal footpath which is uneven in parts, and field

Start point: Car park at North Sands (GR SX 730382)

Parking: North Sands Car Park, Cliff Road, Salcombe (TQ8 8LD)

Dog Friendly: Should be kept on a lead near livestock and on the road

Public toilets: On Cliff Road, east of car park. Also along the route at South Sands Car Park.

Nearest food: The Winking Prawn, next to North Sands Car Park. Lots of cafés in and around Salcombe. In fine weather take a picnic to Sharp Tor

SALCOMBE WALK

1. The walk begins in North Sands Car Park. Leave the car park with the beach in front of you. To the left-hand side of the cliff are the remains of Salcombe Castle, which was heavily involved in the English Civil War. Walk to the right and follow the road uphill. Cliff Road continues uphill and is steep but there are lovely views of Salcombe. The road levels out and then descends into South Sands. There is a small beach here along with cafés, and also a car park, giving an option to start and finish the walk at this point. South Sands is also where the water taxi can be picked up for a ride to Salcombe town centre.

2. At South Sands walk past the beach and hotel. Take the road around to the left which leads uphill giving even more lovely views of Salcombe and the Kingsbridge Estuary. At the post box keep on the road and walk ahead. This leads past Overbeck's where there is a National Trust car park, which gives a further option for starting and finishing this walk.

3. Just past the junction take the footpath marked Starehole Bay. This is uneven and has some beautiful views of the coastline. In wet weather this path is likely to be slippery. The path leads around the coastline and is undulating, up and down steps. You will pass the interestingly named Stink Cove and some dramatic rock formations. The path continues along the coast to Starehole Cove.

4. At the small footbridge take a right turn inland. Walk up the hill to a kissing gate. Go through the gate and take the footpath to the right past an outbuilding. Go through a gate and take the path just ahead on the right. Go through another gate and take the gate at the bottom right corner of this field. This leads out onto the upper cliff path.

5. Follow the fingerpost directions to the viewing point above Sharp Tor where there are magnificent coastal views. There are seats along this part of the trail which make good picnic spots in fine weather.

6. Follow the path around to the left with views of Salcombe Harbour. After passing the triangulation point the footpath splits. Take the right path downhill past Overbeck's, which makes an interesting detour. It continues downhill retracing the route to South Sands and North Sands Beach.

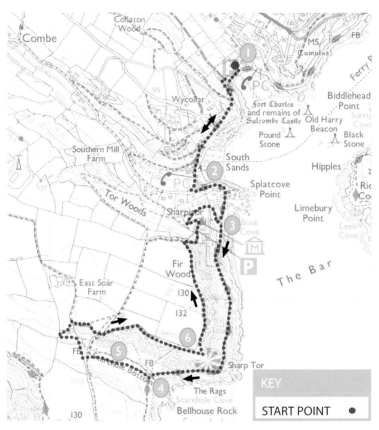

KEY

START POINT ●

START POINT

This walk heads out from the car park east of Start Farm to the lighthouse at Start Point and round the coastal footpath then back to the car park. With planning the walk can be timed to coincide with a visit to the lighthouse, which is open periodically.

Start is Anglo-Saxon for a tail, and considering the long exposed strip of coast where the lighthouse sits it is a good description for this rocky outcrop. Start Point is one of the most exposed areas of coastline in Britain and is generally a wild and windy place. There is evidence all around of the power of the sea here. Just off Start Point is a sandbank called The Skerries. This stretches for four miles (6.5km) off the shore and is made of sand and shell. It lies at a depth of six feet (2 metres) during low tide and affects the way the waves hit the shoreline. In the 18th century the village of Strete Undercliffe was swept into the sea, followed by Hallsands in 1917; the latter the result of a combination of the power of the sea and the Royal Navy taking tons of gravel to build a new dockyard in Plymouth despite local concerns.

The notorious Blackstone Rock has been the cause of many wrecks here. In 1891 the Liverpool barque *Dryad* sank off Start Point in a blizzard with the loss of all hands. The Start Point Lighthouse has been guiding shipping for over 150 years. It was designed in 1837 and has a battlement appearance which was typical of the time. Start Point Lighthouse has been automated since 1993.

iStock

THE BASICS

Distance: 2 miles / 3.2km

Gradient: Mainly flat with an uphill path from the lighthouse

Severity: Generally well marked but there are some uneven rocky parts to the coastal footpath

Approx. time to walk: 1 hour

Stiles: None, but several gates on the walk

Maps: OS Explorer OL20 (South Devon)

Path description: Tarmacked path to the lighthouse, coastal footpath which may be slippery in wet weather. For visits to the lighthouse the Trinity House website displays opening times (www.trinityhouse.co.uk)

Start point: Car park on lane to Start Point (GR SX 821375)

Parking: Car Park on lane to Start Point Lighthouse (TQ7 2ET)

Dog Friendly: Keep on a lead near livestock

Public toilets: One toilet in the Start Point car park courtesy of the car park attendant

Nearest food: None locally. The Cricket Inn at Beesands is a short drive away

START POINT WALK

1. Begin the walk in the Start Point car park where there is an interesting information board about the area. On a clear day there is a magnificent view of the coastline including the destroyed village of Hallsands. The Day Mark Tower that guides shipping into Dartmouth can be spotted from here and sometimes the outline of Portland Island in Dorset is visible. The white waves about a mile offshore mark The Skerries, the famous sandbank. Go through the gate to the right of the car park. Follow this path down to a footpath sign.

2. Continue walking down the path towards the lighthouse. There are some lovely views of the coastline from here. The tower stands 92 feet (28 metres) high and the range of light is 25 nautical miles. During fog a horn sounds every 60 seconds. From the lighthouse retrace your steps to the footpath sign which displays the distance of the starting and finishing points of the South West Coastal Footpath at Poole and Minehead. Take the path to the left and walk over The Warren, taking care as the path descends to a track. Turn right and follow this path along the coast. This section of the path is covered in wild flowers and is renowned for its bluebells in spring. Keep an eye out for seals as they are often spotted along this coastal section.

3. Walk past the sign marked Gull Island. Continue on the path. There are sections that are quite rocky here, which could be slippery in wet weather. This continues past Peartree Point. Historically wrecking is said to have taken place along this coastline.

4. Just before Great Mattiscombe Beach there is a footpath signpost indicating Start Point in an inland direction. Take the path to the right that leads uphill. This goes through several wooden gates and continues uphill through a sheltered valley. Eventually this path emerges at the car park gate and the start of the walk. Another option for walkers is to visit the deserted village of Hallsands which is just north of Start Point.

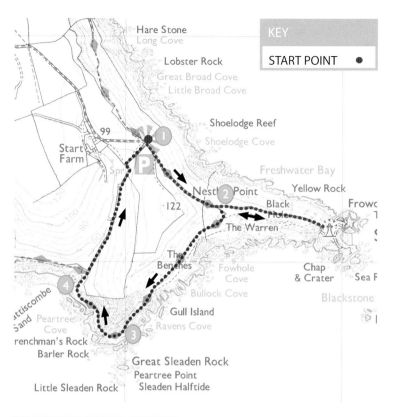

KEY

START POINT •

TIVERTON

THIS WALK STARTS IN TIVERTON AND LEADS THROUGH THE
OUTSKIRTS OF TOWN BEFORE RETURNING VIA THE TOWPATH
ON THE GRAND WESTERN CANAL.

The Grand Western Canal was originally intended to link Bristol with the English Channel, but this dream was never completed. Originally the plans were to link the Exeter Canal with the new Grand Western and plans were approved in 1796. The route was surveyed by John Rennie with work beginning on the summit stretch in 1810 until completion in 1814. Eventually the canal linked Tiverton with Taunton and was 11 miles (18km) long and further work was carried out on other stretches of the route but it never joined the English Channel with Bristol as originally intended. The plans for the canal were superseded by the railways as the Industrial Revolution progressed.

Lime kilns were built alongside the canal basin in 1829 and the waterway was an effective transportation system for both this and for coal. The kilns were fed directly from the barges, and farmers used the lime as fertiliser. These kilns were in use until the 1890s and acted as a hub for people to gather and chat. Boys roasted potatoes in the kilns and beggars slept by them to keep warm.

During the 1960s there was a lily growing trade around the canal but as it silted up this ceased. From 1974 the area became a nature reserve and the canal is renowned for its traditional horse-drawn barge; the last of its kind in South West England.

THE BASICS

Distance: 3 miles / 4.8km

Gradient: Mainly flat

Severity: Easy

Approx. time to walk: 1–1½ hours

Stiles: None but two sets of steps

Maps: OS Explorer 114 (Exeter & The Exe Valley)

Path description: Road, footpath, canal towpath. Please note that the horse has priority over all other canal users and walkers should keep clear when the barge is in use on the canal

Start point: Grand Western Canal Country Park (GR SS 964124)

Parking: Grand Western Canal Country Park, Tiverton (EX16 4HX)

Dog Friendly: Yes but keep on a lead on the road. Not permitted on the horse-drawn barge

Public toilets: In the car park

Nearest food: Canal Tea Rooms and Garden in the car park. There is also a floating café on the canal

1. Leave the Grand Western Canal Country Park Car Park and head towards the main road. Before doing so take time to look at the remains of the old lime kilns and the quarry stones. Having a waterside location for these historic kilns improved the efficiency of the trade here. At the junction with the road, turn right. Walk downhill, which gives views across the town centre.

2. At the corner of the road turn right and continue walking downhill. Take the road that veers to the right past a white building named the Old Road Depot and some Victorian-style houses. The road now road leads past a small park and some open areas. Look for the cycle trail path ahead.

3. Walk down the marked cycle path (National Cycle Path No. 3) past houses. There are wild flowers along this path. At the railway arch take the steps to the right of the bridge which lead to the road. At the road turn right. Just ahead is a Victorian post box on the wall. Continue walking up the road and around a corner. On the left-hand side of the road are some steps. These lead to the canal.

4. On the canal towpath turn right and follow the path back to Tiverton Basin. This stretch of waterway is a nature reserve and there are moorhen, swans, kingfishers and several other species of bird. In total there are 24 bridges along the Grand Western Canal. Many are Grade II listed buildings and were

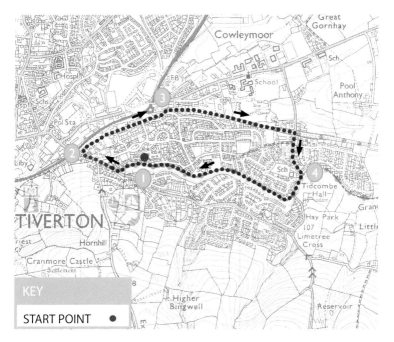

built by the canal architect John Rennie. This walk passes just a few of these bridges. Back at Tiverton Basin there is a visitor centre which tells the history of the canal and the lime kilns. There is also a gift shop that sells tickets for the horse-drawn barge trip which operates from April to October and is a pleasant way to round off the walk.

UFFCULME

This short walk starts in the centre of Uffculme village and continues along the picturesque bank of the River Culm. It includes an optional visit to one of the oldest working woollen mill museums in the world to see the distinctive cloth being made.

Uffculme is a small village in Mid Devon just off the busy M5. It lies on the River Culm and from the 16th century was at the centre of the woollen industry in Devon. The quality of wool produced in Devon was recognised internationally. Exeter was at the centre of the wool industry and was where serges and cloth were traded. Many villagers spun wool in their homes, but as the Industrial Revolution progressed mills became more of a feature on the landscape. During the 18th century this area exported large quantities of Uffculme serge to countries like Holland. In 1797 Thomas Fox, from the prominent Cornish Quaker family, purchased the site and constructed Coldharbour Mill, which was in constant production until 1981.

Today Coldharbour Mill has been restored as a working woollen mill museum and is open to the public. The heritage of the woollen industry in England is illustrated by the Woolsack on which the Lord Chancellor sits. Water is integral to wool production for washing and also in driving the early machinery used for tucking and weaving. The River Culm flows quietly today, with weirs and wildlife, but two centuries ago was a busy area at the heart of the woollen trade. The shop at the mill sells four distinctive tartans including Blackdown Hills and Green Devon designs and a variety of other woollen products. The mill's website, with opening times and details of special events such as steam-ups, is www.coldharbourmill.org.uk.

THE BASICS

Distance: 2 miles / 3.2km

Gradient: Flat

Severity: An easy walk

Approx. time to walk: 1 hour with additional time to tour the mill

Stiles: None

Maps: OS Explorer 128 (Taunton & Blackdown Hills)

Path description: Road and footpath

Start point: The Square, Uffculme (GR ST 068127)

Parking: The Square, Uffculme (EX15 3AA)

Dog Friendly: Not allowed in the mill. Keep on a lead on the road and near livestock.

Public toilets: On Highland Terrace just off Commercial Road in the Uffculme Bowling Club

Nearest food: Ostler Inn; village shop sells snacks; restaurant at Coldharbour Mill

UFFCULME WALK

1. Start in the village square where the shelter and bench marks what was the old Shambles. This acted as a cattle market until World War I and is believed to have been a trading point for serges and cloth in the 16th century. Walk towards the church, St Mary's, which dates from medieval times. Take the road on the right past the church towards the river. At the bridge cross the river and take the footpath to the right.

2. Walk along the river bank on the footpath. There are small weirs along the river and kingfishers are sometimes spotted here. Continue walking towards a bridge.

3. Take the steps beside the bridge to the road and turn right. There are further weirs on the right and a metal gate leads to the old Tiverton to Hemyock railway line, now disused. Continue walking up towards Coldharbour Mill, which is distinguished by its brick chimney stack and the large building. It is one of the oldest woollen mills in the world and now operates as a working museum. Coldharbour Mill displays its opening times on its website and offers self-guided tours or special 'steam up' days on public holidays. There is an admission charge to tour the mill and it is closed at weekends. **Coldharbour** comes from the Saxon word **Columb**, which means a cold valley. Uffculme would have been a place to shelter for pilgrims en route to St Patrick's Well at nearby Dunkeswell. The site with its water power and wool industry was the ideal place for Thomas Fox to build the mill in 1797. From the mill continue walking up the road, following it around to the left. Walk ahead to the main road and turn right. Walk along the road keeping on the pavements as the road can be busy. This passes houses and leads back into Uffculme where the walk began.

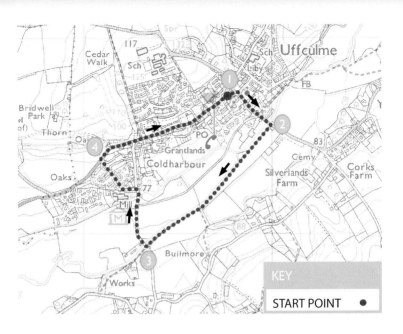

WESTWARD HO!

THIS WALK BEGINS ALONG THE DRAMATIC SOUTH WEST COAST FOOTPATH ALONG THE WESTWARD HO! COAST BEFORE HEADING INLAND TO PICTURESQUE COUNTRYSIDE LANES. IT RETURNS TO WESTWARD HO! VIA KIPLING TORS AND EXPLORES SOME OF THE QUIETER PARTS OF THE AREA, AWAY FROM THE MAIN RESORT.

In 1855 the adventure novel **Westward Ho!** was published by Charles Kingsley and featured Amyas Leigh, a boy who follows Sir Francis Drake to sea. Kingsley had been inspired by the magnificent coastline and tales of local seafarers who frequented the area, and he wrote the novel whilst staying in nearby Bideford. It is a book renowned for its episodes of fighting the Spanish at sea, but Kingsley's descriptions of the North Devon Coast are just as vivid. **Westward Ho!** became a bestseller and fuelled demand by Victorians for holidays around North Devon and its coastline. Local entrepreneurs seized the opportunity to develop the area around Northam Burrows. Hotels sprang up, one of them named after the novel, and a railway line circuited the nearby cliffs. To Charles Kingsley's dismay, the whole area soon came to be known as Westward Ho! and quickly developed into a popular seaside holiday resort. It is the only place in the United Kingdom to have an exclamation mark within its spelling.

Westward Ho! was one of the childhood residences of Rudyard Kipling. He attended school here and played in the area around the cliffs. His novel **Stalky & Co.** was published in

1899 based on his experiences at the United Services College. Today Westward Ho! is popular with surfers, walkers and holidaymakers. It is famous for the massive Pebble Ridge of boulders which prevents erosion of the Northam Burrows and the two-mile (3km) stretch of golden sands.

THE BASICS

Distance: 4 miles / 6.4km

Gradient: One steep ascent, otherwise fairly undulating

Severity: An easy walk

Approx. time to walk: 2–3 hours

Stiles: Two

Maps: OS Explorer 139 (Bideford, Ilfracombe & Barnstaple)

Path description: Coastal footpath and road

Start point: Seafield car park (GR SS 423291)

Parking: Seafield long stay car park (EX39 1JS)

Dog Friendly: Keep on a lead near livestock and on the road

Public toilets: The car park

Nearest food: The Pig on the Hill (booking essential); The Pier House is close to the car park

WESTWARD HO! WALK

1. The walk starts in Seafield Car Park which is adjacent to the South West Coast Footpath. Take the footpath away from the town and walk ahead on the marked track across the cliffs. This was once part of the railway line connecting Abbotsham with Bideford and Appledore. It ran alarmingly close to the coastline and was so popular that people sometimes travelled on the steps. It was requisitioned for military use during World War I. Follow the path along this coastal track where there are magnificent views of the sea. This continues to Cornborough Cliffs where the path runs closer to the sea. Along this coast there are huge pebbles on the beach, which is popular with surfers.

2. At the marked footpath to Abbotsham turn left and cross the stile. Walk across the field and head uphill where the path levels out. Follow the path to a stile. Cross the stile and turn right. Walk down the path to the road.

3. At the road junction turn left. This narrow road continues past the junction for Abbotsham village. Continue past fields and another junction on the left. At the next road junction there are views of Kenwith Castle, an earthwork with a single rampart. It is a natural knoll and believed to be the site of a Saxon castle where the men of Devon defeated the Danes. At the junction marked Whitehouse Cross turn left and use the grass verge to walk on as the road can be busy.

4. Walk up to the curve in the road. Take the smaller road ahead which goes uphill and is signposted Pusehill. This road goes uphill past farmland. It passes the Pig on the Hill pub. As the road levels it arrives at a small junction. Ahead is a marked footpath.

5. Walk through the gate and take the footpath ahead, which runs behind houses. This joins a path that winds downhill on what is known as Kipling Tors. The hill was one of the areas where a young Rudyard Kipling used to play. It is also where Kipling and his friends smoked cigars and pipes whilst reading books. There is an old lookout hut at the top of the hill which has been restored as an art project.

6. At a fork in the paths take the right path downhill. Continue on the path that winds downhill and through trees. Go through the gate at the bottom of the hill past huts. The car park where the walk began is on your left.

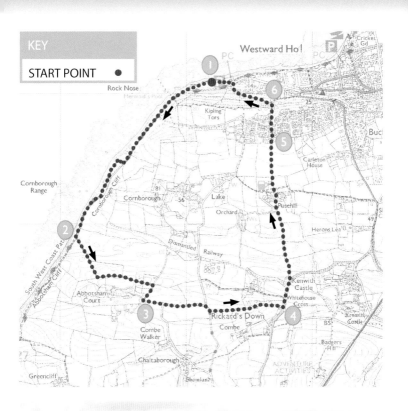

KEY

START POINT ●

WHIMPLE

This circular walk visits the pretty village of Whimple, including traditional cider apple orchards and the surrounding countryside.

In 1897 Whimple had 47 suppliers of apples, which had increased to 1,243 growers by 1929. Many old varieties of apple were grown in and around the village itself. With quaint names like White Sheep's Nose, Fair Maid of Devon and Spotted Dick there was a time when most Devon villages had their own distinctive apple varieties.

In Whimple there are still a few Whimple Wonder cider apple trees. At one time Whiteway's produced cider in Whimple itself and employed many local people. It closed in 1985, moving cider production to Somerset. Today there are houses built on the old factory site but cider orchards are still worked here. Apple juice is produced in the village. On 17 January each year the village celebrates Wassailing in the orchards when the trees are toasted and the traditional verse is recited:

> Here's to thee, old apple tree,
> That blooms well, bears well.
> Hats full, caps full,
> Three bushel bags full,
> An' all under one tree.
> Hurrah! Hurrah!

The Whimple Heritage Centre has a fascinating display of the old cider producers and other village and rural items including a barrel-making machine. Whimple was home to Ann Hogarth, the creator of Muffin the Mule, and the Heritage Centre has a display about this famous TV character.

THE BASICS

Distance: 4 miles / 4.6km

Gradient: Mainly flat with one steep and uneven footpath

Severity: Easy

Approx. time to walk: 2 hours

Stiles: Four

Maps: OS Explorer 115 (Exmouth & Sidmouth)

Path description: Road, footpaths, orchards

Start point: Whimple Church (GR SY 044972)

Parking: Car park on Webber Close (EX5 2SP)

Dog Friendly: Keep on leads on the road and near livestock

Public toilets: None

Nearest food: Thirsty Farmer Pub; New Fountain Pub; the village shop sells locally produced apple juice and snacks

WHIMPLE WALK

1. The walk starts at the parish church in Whimple, which dates back to Norman times. Walk towards the post office and continue on the road around to the left. Continue walking down this road towards the station.

2. Take the footpath on the right towards Whimple Station. If arriving in Whimple by train the walk could be started and finished at this point. From the station walk up to the main road and turn left. Walk down this road and past the Thirsty Farmer pub.

3. At the mini roundabout take the narrow road ahead. This curves around to the right and goes uphill towards Knowle Cross. At a junction with the road, turn left. Walk down this road to a footpath on the left.

4. Cross the stile and walk across the orchard. Depending on the time of year the trees may be in blossom or have fruit. Keep on the footpath and walk to the next stile which is in the bottom right corner of the field. Cross the stile. In the next field turn left and cross a stile into the next field. Walk through this field to a stile and cross it. Follow the footpath which leads to the road. Cross the road and take the footpath ahead which runs behind houses. Go through a kissing gate and over a wooden footbridge. Walk towards a railway arch. Go under the arch and walk on the path past houses and out onto the road. Turn left and walk through the village centre.

5. At the village stores turn right and walk up to Whimple Heritage Centre on the right. This is full of interesting information about the village and is worth a stop either at the beginning or middle of the walk. Continue walking on the road, taking care as there is no pavement. Walk past a road junction signposted Woodhayes. At the permissive way marked Plumtree Lane turn left.

6. Walk down this lane, which has orchard fields on either side. Further up this lane is a narrow path which leads steeply downhill and is uneven. This may be slippery in wet weather. Take this path downhill to a road junction and turn right.

7. Continue along this road past farmhouses. Take the first road on the left. This road curves around and leads back into Whimple where the walk began.

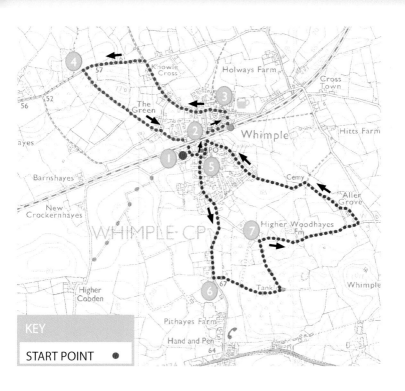

ABOUT THE AUTHOR

Rachael Rowe is a writer specialising in travel and health and lives in Dorset. Her publications include online and print travel articles. Walking is a particular interest and the area in North Dorset where she lives is full of places to roam. She also works in the NHS, specialising in cardiovascular disease, and is fully aware of the benefits of walking for health.

Rachael is originally from Cornwall and has travelled to over 50 countries, many with classic walking trails, and has also lived in Switzerland. The West Country is a particular favourite place to walk on weekends and she has enjoyed creating this book so that others can get out and about and discover what Devon has to offer.

Her portfolio can be seen at www.rachaelrowe.com